PowerPhonics™

The Red Rose

Learning the R Sound

Ilse Battistoni

The Rosen Publishing Group's
PowerKids Press™
New York

A red rose is a flower.

3

Red roses grow in the garden.

Red roses grow in a row.

Red roses grow by the road.

Red roses grow by my house.

Red roses need rain to grow.

Red roses need sun to grow.

Mom cuts the red roses.

I have red roses in my room.

I like red roses.

Word List

rain

red

road

room

rose

row

Instructional Guide

Note to Instructors:
One of the essential skills that enable a young child to read is the ability to associate letter-sound symbols and blend these sounds to form words. Phonics instruction can teach children a system that will help them decode unfamiliar words and, in turn, enhance their word-recognition skills. We offer a phonics-based series of books that are easy to read and understand. Each book pairs words and pictures that reinforce specific phonetic sounds in a logical sequence. Topics are based on curriculum goals appropriate for early readers in the areas of science, social studies, and health.

Letter/Sound: r – Have the child tell what vowel sounds they hear in the following words: *run, rabbit, rags, rock, rob, red, rug, rest, rub, ring, rat, rip.* As the child responds, list the words on a chalkboard or dry-erase board. Ask: "How are all of these words alike?" Have the child underline the initial **r** in each word.
- Have the child refer to the word list to find out which vowel is in the most **r** words. Which is in the fewest? How many words have only three letters? How many have more than three letters?

Phonics Activities: Have the child name initial **r** words that rhyme with: *fun, sing, toad, boom, nose, dust, tub, sock, test, bug.* As the child responds, list both the initial **r** word and its matching rhyming word. Ask the child to compare word endings.
- Arrange the following phrase cards on a table: *in the road, in a ring, on a rock, on a rug, on the run, in a row.* Display and read aloud the following sentence starters, one at a time, and have the child complete them using one of the above phrases: *A hopping toad is _____; A little bug is _____; A yellow sock is _____; We sing and sing _____; We have fun _____; Roses grow _____.*
- Provide a work sheet containing the following incomplete initial **r** words: *r__n, r__g, r__ck, r__t, r__b, r__d, r__p, r__m.* Have the child choose a vowel for each group of letters to make a word. Ask them to use the words in sentences.

Additional Resources:
- Bunting, Eve. *Flower Garden*. San Diego, CA: Harcourt, 1999.
- Heller, Ruth. *The Reason for a Flower*. New York: The Putnam Publishing Group, 1999.
- Saunders, Gail. *Flowers*. Danbury, CT: Children's Press, 1998.
- Schaefer, Lola M. *Honey Bees & Flowers*. Mankato, MN: Capstone Press, Inc., 1999.

Published in 2002 by The Rosen Publishing Group, Inc.
29 East 21st Street, New York, NY 10010

Copyright © 2002 by The Rosen Publishing Group, Inc.

Book Design: Haley Wilson

Photo Credits: Cover, p. 3 © Peter Langone/International Stock; pp. 5, 13 © ChromaZone Images/Index Stock; p. 7 © Roberto Soncin Gerometta/Photo 20-20/PictureQuest; p. 9 © Scott Barrow/International Stock; p. 11 © Gay Bumgarner/Index Stock; pp. 15, 19 © Eric Kamp/Index Stock; p. 17 © Corbis; p. 21 © Peter Stone/Black Star Publishing/PictureQuest.

Library of Congress Cataloging-in-Publication Data

Battistoni, Ilse.
    The red rose : learning the R sound / Ilse Battistoni.— 1st ed.
        p. cm. — (Power phonics/phonics for the real world)
    ISBN 0-8239-5912-0 (lib. bdg. : alk. paper)
    ISBN 0-8239-8257-2 (pbk. : alk. paper)
    6-pack ISBN 0-8239-9225-X
    1. Roses—Juvenile literature. 2. English
    language—Consonants—Juvenile literature. [1. Roses.] I. Title.
    II. Series.
    SB411 .B354 2002
    635.9'33734—dc21
                                            2001000192

Manufactured in the United States of America